HANDBOOK
FOR THE
RECENTLY
DECEASED

ISBN: 978-5299688313

We gratefully acknowledge the following for the material and assistance they have provided: Warner Bros. Pictures.

This book is a replica of the original Handbook for the Recently Deceased as seen in the 1988 film Beetlejuice.

The cover and the first few pages of this book have been painstakingly recreated using a genuine prop which was used for filming as a reference.

There were several identical Handbook props made for the film, all of which were created using a psychology textbook as a template.

Since no actual content exists for the body of the rest of these pages, the remainder of this book has been cleared for you to use as a journal or sketchbook should you wish.

This book consists of 60 lined pages on a cream background with title.

Perfect for any Tim Burton or 80's movie fan.

This Book Belongs To:
____
____
____

HANDBOOK FOR THE RECENTLY DECEASED

HANDBOOK FOR THE RECENTLY DECEASED

HANDBOOK FOR THE RECENTLY DECEASED

HANDBOOK FOR THE RECENTLY DECEASED

HANDBOOK FOR THE RECENTLY DECEASED

HANDBOOK FOR THE RECENTLY DECEASED

HANDBOOK FOR THE RECENTLY DECEASED

HANDBOOK FOR THE RECENTLY DECEASED

HANDBOOK FOR THE RECENTLY DECEASED

HANDBOOK FOR THE RECENTLY DECEASED

HANDBOOK FOR THE RECENTLY DECEASED

HANDBOOK FOR THE RECENTLY DECEASED

HANDBOOK FOR THE RECENTLY DECEASED

HANDBOOK FOR THE RECENTLY DECEASED

HANDBOOK FOR THE RECENTLY DECEASED

HANDBOOK FOR THE RECENTLY DECEASED

HANDBOOK FOR THE RECENTLY DECEASED

HANDBOOK FOR THE RECENTLY DECEASED

HANDBOOK FOR THE RECENTLY DECEASED

HANDBOOK FOR THE RECENTLY DECEASED

HANDBOOK FOR THE RECENTLY DECEASED

HANDBOOK FOR THE RECENTLY DECEASED

HANDBOOK FOR THE RECENTLY DECEASED

HANDBOOK FOR THE RECENTLY DECEASED

HANDBOOK FOR THE RECENTLY DECEASED

HANDBOOK FOR THE RECENTLY DECEASED

HANDBOOK FOR THE RECENTLY DECEASED

HANDBOOK FOR THE RECENTLY DECEASED

HANDBOOK FOR THE RECENTLY DECEASED

HANDBOOK FOR THE RECENTLY DECEASED

HANDBOOK FOR THE RECENTLY DECEASED

HANDBOOK FOR THE RECENTLY DECEASED

HANDBOOK FOR THE RECENTLY DECEASED

HANDBOOK FOR THE RECENTLY DECEASED

HANDBOOK FOR THE RECENTLY DECEASED

HANDBOOK FOR THE RECENTLY DECEASED

HANDBOOK FOR THE RECENTLY DECEASED

HANDBOOK FOR THE RECENTLY DECEASED

HANDBOOK FOR THE RECENTLY DECEASED

HANDBOOK FOR THE RECENTLY DECEASED

HANDBOOK FOR THE RECENTLY DECEASED

HANDBOOK FOR THE RECENTLY DECEASED